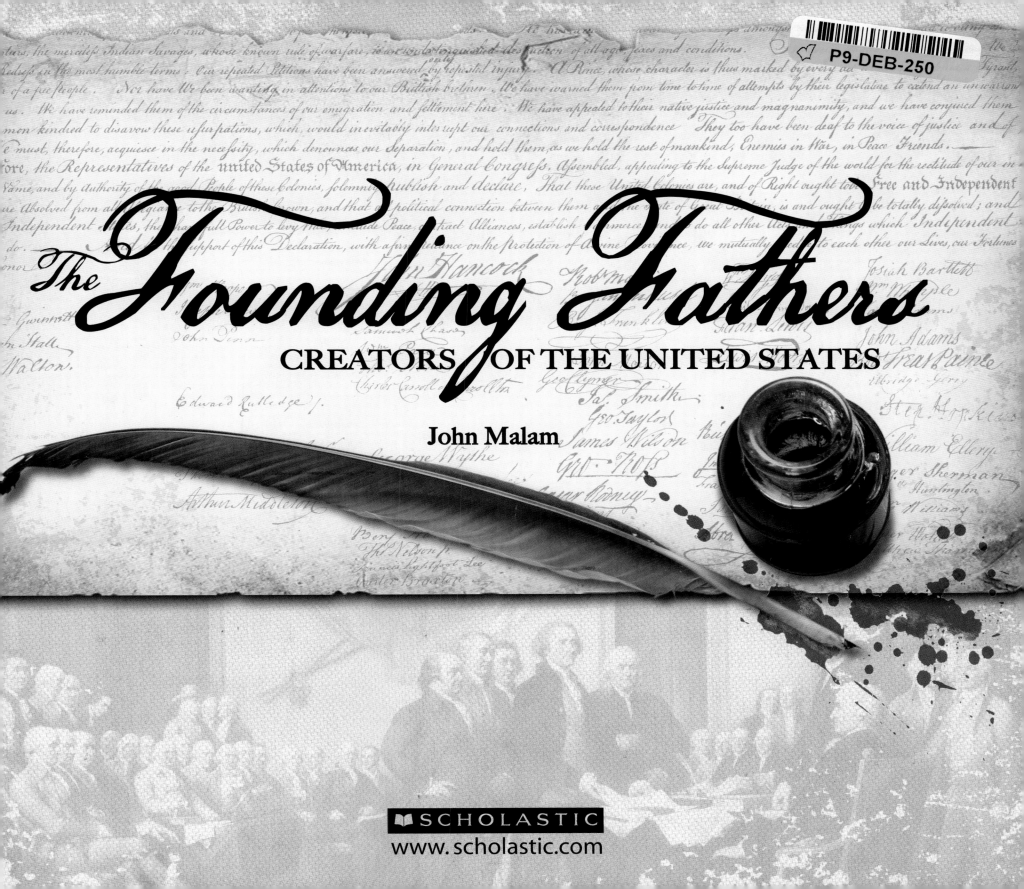

The Founding Fathers

CREATORS OF THE UNITED STATES

John Malam

SCHOLASTIC
www.scholastic.com

Introduction

Their names and reputations have made history: George Washington, James Madison, John Adams, Alexander Hamilton, Thomas Jefferson, and Benjamin Franklin. These are some of the men who shaped one of the greatest nations on Earth. They are the Founding Fathers of the United States of America.

The story of the Founding Fathers of the United States is one of determination against the odds. The Founding Fathers were determined to break free from the grip of a colonial power to create a new nation, by the people, for the people. This is their story.

Benjamin Franklin

One of the most important of the Founding Fathers was Benjamin Franklin (1706–1790). He was a statesman, diplomat, writer, scientist, and inventor, and one of the most talented men of his time.

A leading figure in the struggle for independence from Great Britain, Franklin helped draft the Declaration of Independence and was one of its signers in 1776. He represented the US in France during the American Revolutionary War (1775–1783), signed the Treaty of Paris that ended the war (1783), and was a delegate to the Constitutional Convention, which created the Constitution of the United States—a document Franklin also signed (1787).

At the age of 81, Franklin was the Convention's oldest delegate, and has been hailed as "the First American."

Benjamin Franklin is one of the most important Americans ever to have lived.

"Either write something worth reading or do something worth writing."
—attributed to Benjamin Franklin

"He is a most extraordinary man ..."
—William Pierce, a member of the Constitutional Convention, describing Benjamin Franklin

Birth of a Nation

There are some dates in history that have changed the world. The 4th of July, 1776, is one of those incredible dates. On that day, the U.S. declared its **independence** from Great Britain. It was a giant step toward becoming an independent nation. However, Britain was not going to let its North American **colonies** go free without a fight.

COLONY	DATE FOUNDED
Virginia	1607
Massachusetts	1620
New Hampshire	1623
Connecticut	1633
Maryland	1634
Rhode Island	1636
Delaware	1638
North Carolina	1663
New Jersey	1664
New York	1664
South Carolina	1670
Pennsylvania	1681
Georgia	1733

Thirteen colonies

By the mid-1700s, about two million people lived in Great Britain's North American colonies. There were thirteen colonies, stretched along the eastern seaboard of North America, south of present-day Canada. The colonies were ruled by Britain from Britain, and for many people in the colonies, that was a problem. To them, they were Americans, and Britain was a foreign country far away that had no right to interfere in their affairs. The colonies grew restless, and rebelled in Massachusetts. As a result, the British government sent its army to restore British control.

The Revolutionary War

On April 19, 1775, British troops were stopped by armed American patriots near Concord, Massachusetts. The British ordered the Americans to lay down their arms, but they refused. It's not clear who fired the first shot, but it was the shot that started the American Revolutionary War. This was a bitter war, fought over six years between Great Britain and her American colonies.

Declaration of Independence

As the war entered its second year, American politicians began talking about independence—freedom—from Great Britain. At first, some colonies did not want to break away, but after more talks they were all in favor, and the Declaration of Independence was adopted on July 4, 1776. This day later became known as "Independence Day."

The Declaration of Independence

Britain surrenders

Both sides had victories and setbacks during the Revolutionary War, but by the autumn of 1781, British forces were besieged at Yorktown, Virginia. The war ended on October 19, 1781, when British troops surrendered to General George Washington. Two years later, on September 3, 1783, a peace document known as the **Treaty** of Paris was signed, and the Revolutionary War officially ended. The thirteen colonies had gained their freedom from Great Britain, and they became the first states in a new nation: the United States of America.

An early version of the US flag, with seven red and six white stripes and 13 stars in a blue field. The stars represented the original 13 states.

Continental Congress

Before the first shot was fired in the American Revolutionary War, a different kind of war was raging between Great Britain and her colonies. It was a war of words between politicians from both sides. The "word war" united the thirteen American colonies against Britain, and from it emerged strong leaders and the first signs of a national, or **federal**, government.

American patriots disguised as Mohawks (a Native American people) throw 342 chests of tea into Boston Harbor.

Road to revolution

In 1767, many everyday goods in America began to cost more because the British government added a **tax** onto them. Americans protested, and people stopped buying British goods. In 1770, Britain scrapped taxes on all goods except tea. The tea tax was unpopular, and in 1773, chests of British tea were thrown into Boston Harbor, Massachusetts, by American protestors. The British government was outraged by the "Boston Tea Party," as it was later called, and passed laws to punish Boston (called the "Coercive" or "Intolerable Acts").

"The present unhappy state"

For many Americans, Great Britain had gone too far. It was bad enough to be paying tax to Britain, but the presence of thousands of British soldiers only made matters worse. American newspapers and **pamphlets** called for independence from Britain. In September 1774, delegates from twelve of the thirteen colonies came together for the First Continental Congress. Only those from Georgia stayed away. The meeting, held in Philadelphia, Pennsylvania, was called "to consult upon the present unhappy state of the colonies."

A British officer being harassed by colonial boys in Boston.

The colonies' demands

After seven weeks of talks, the First Continental Congress ended, and the colonies made their demands to Britain. The colonies wanted British troops pulled out of Boston and the Coercive Acts repealed. Until that happened, the colonies refused to trade with Great Britain. They made a plan to meet again in eight months if the British did not meet their demands. Britain refused the colonies' demands and sent troops to end what was seen as a **rebellion** in Massachusetts.

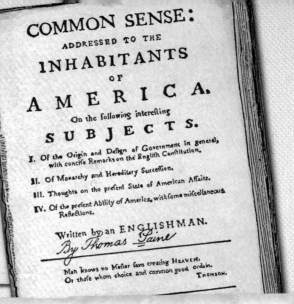

COMMON SENSE:
ADDRESSED TO THE
INHABITANTS
OF
AMERICA.
On the following interesting
SUBJECTS.

I. Of the Origin and Design of Government in general, with concise Remarks on the English Constitution.
II. Of Monarchy and Hereditary Succession.
III. Thoughts on the present State of American Affairs.
IV. Of the present Ability of America, with some miscellaneous Reflections.

Written by an ENGLISHMAN.
By Thomas Paine

Man knows no Master save creating HEAVEN,
Or those whom choice and common good ordain.
THOMSON.

Common Sense, Thomas Paine's pamphlet published in 1776. It inspired people in the colonies to declare independence from Britain.

The Declaration of Independence was drafted at the Second Continental Congress.

"Put into a state of defence"

The Second Continental Congress went ahead as planned in Philadelphia in May 1775. All thirteen colonies were represented—and this time there was a war to discuss, because the first shots in the American Revolution had been fired that April. Right away, Congress agreed that the colonies "be immediately put into a state of defence." Plans were made to raise a Continental Army of 20,000 men, with George Washington as its commander.

Strong leaders emerge

The Continental Congress met at different towns throughout the six years of fighting. Powerful leaders emerged, including George Washington (Virginia), Thomas Jefferson (Virginia), Benjamin Franklin (Pennsylvania), Patrick Henry (Virginia), James Madison (Virginia), and John Adams (Massachusetts). These, and others, were to become the Founding Fathers of the United States.

The First Continental Congress.

Congress appointed George Washington as commander-in-chief of the Continental Army.

George Washington, War Hero

As early as 1778, George Washington was described as the "Father of His Country." The American Revolutionary War was still being fought, and it was to be another five years before the United States of America could call itself an independent nation, completely free of British control.

Raised to be a tobacco farmer

George Washington was born in 1732, on his parents' tobacco **plantation** in Virginia. He studied English, mathematics, and geography at school, but as the son of a farmer, his "real education" did not come from books. Instead, the young Washington learned how to be a tobacco farmer, like his father, grandfather, and great-grandfather before him.

George Washington as a young man.

Mount Vernon estate

Washington's older brother, Lawrence, was in charge of the family tobacco plantation at Mount Vernon, Virginia. When Lawrence died in 1752, Mount Vernon was passed on to George. Aged just 20, he was now head of one of Virginia's wealthiest estates. For the next 20 years, Washington farmed his Mount Vernon estate. He enlarged the main house, increased the size of the estate to 8,000 acres, and bought slaves to work the land.

The French and Indian War

Starting in 1754, Great Britain and France fought each other over control of North America, where both nations had colonies, in what became known as the French and Indian War. Washington fought for the British. His military career had begun, and in 1755, aged 23, he was made commander of Britain's colonial troops in Virginia. His life was nearly cut short when four enemy bullets ripped through his coat and two horses were shot from under him. The fighting ended in 1760, when Britain won. Washington had proven himself to be a natural leader. After the war, he returned to his life as a farmer at Mount Vernon.

The British surrender in 1781.

The Revolutionary War

The peace that followed the French and Indian War was short-lived. To pay for the war, Great Britain increased the taxes paid by her American colonies. The colonies protested, and the American Revolutionary War followed in April 1775 as a result. That May, all thirteen colonies sent **representatives** to the Second Continental Congress, which met in Philadelphia. The state of Virginia sent George Washington. Having shown his skills as a general in the French and Indian War, Washington was **elected** commander-in-chief of the Continental Army. He took charge of an ill-trained army that lacked leadership, but under his command he turned it into a disciplined fighting force.

The armed struggle against Britain lasted six grueling years. Finally, in 1781, Washington forced British General Charles Cornwallis to surrender at Yorktown, Virginia. Two years later, the last British troops left American soil.

The mansion was enlarged to a 21-bedroom residence by Washington over a period of 45 years.

Retires to Mount Vernon

The war had ended in victory for the colonies, and Washington became a national hero. In December 1783, he announced that his army life was over—his job was finished. He planned to return to his Mount Vernon home and his "other life" as a farmer. But his country would not let him go that easily; there was still work for George Washington to do as a new nation began to emerge.

Articles of Confederation

A significant act of the Continental Congress during the American Revolutionary War was the creation of the Articles of **Confederation**. This was the first attempt at creating a written **constitution**, setting America on course toward its first national government.

The first page of the Articles of Confederation.

John Dickinson (1732-1808)

Penman of the Revolution

The Articles of Confederation, which were **drafted** in June 1776, were largely the work of John Dickinson (Pennsylvania). He was known as the "Penman of the Revolution" because of the many official documents he had already written for the Continental Congress. He was also one of the best legal minds in the colonies. Dickinson wanted the thirteen colonies to join together to form a "firm league of friendship," or a confederation.

Toward a national government

The articles granted important powers to the Continental Congress, which allowed it to act like a national, or federal, government of all the colonies. Congress could:

- send **ambassadors** to foreign countries;
- issue money;
- borrow money;
- set up a postal system;
- declare war;
- make treaties;
- control the affairs of Native Americans;
- keep an army and a navy;
- call on the colonies to provide troops and money in time of war;
- set standards for weights and measures; and
- settle boundary disputes between colonies

JOIN, or DIE.

Distrust of national government

The Articles of Confederation were supposed to create one government for all the colonies. However, that raised a problem. At the time the articles were drafted, the colonies were fighting for their independence from an all-controlling government (Britain). Would a national American government be any better, or would it upset the colonies by interfering in their internal affairs? Because there was a distrust of national authority, the Articles of Confederation got off to a bad start, and it was not until 1781 that all thirteen colonies agreed to adopt them.

A famous political cartoon, created by Benjamin Franklin. It shows a snake cut into pieces, the pieces representing the different colonies. The message to the colonies was clear: join together to act as one body, or die.

Continental dollars, issued by different colonies during the American Revolution.

Continental dollars

During the American Revolutionary War, the Continental Congress issued paper money known as "Continental currency." Each colony issued its own money in dollars, which were used to pay the troops of the Continental Army and buy goods. In total, Congress issued $241,552,780 in Continental currency.

However, because Congress did not have the same value held in gold or silver to back up the paper money, the new currency quickly lost its value. To make matters worse, the British government put fake dollar bills into circulation.

By May 1781, Continental dollars had become so worthless that they ceased to circulate as money. Any worthless object was described as "not worth a Continental."

The Constitutional Convention

By the mid-1780s, it was clear to many Americans that the Articles of Confederation were not working. The thirteen original states were looking after their own internal affairs, leaving the fledgling nation with a weak federal government. The states were not united as one nation. Something had to be done, and it began with a quarrel between Maryland and Virginia.

The states of Maryland and Virginia, separated by the Potomac River.

Potomac River dispute

The Potomac River flows between the states of Maryland and Virginia. However, instead of being divided down the middle, which is how river borders are usually agreed, Maryland had been granted the whole of the river. This upset Virginia, which wanted an equal share. The federal government had no powers to intervene.

James Madison (1751–1836)

An idea takes shap

Before the Maryland–Virginia quarrel got out of hand, James Madison sugges that officials from both states get toget to work out a solution. This discussion between the two states took place at George Washington's Mount Vernon estate in March 1785. As a next step, they decided to include Pennsylvania in future talks. Seeing how the states were cooperating with each other gave Madison a new idea. He wondered if all thirteen states could agree on forming federal government. In September 1786 five states met in Annapolis, Maryland They proposed that all states should se **delegates** to a meeting in Philadelphia the following year.

James Madison's **essay**, "Vices of the Political System."

James Madison: a man with a plan

James Madison gave a lot of thought to the idea of a federal government. A few weeks before the meeting in Philadelphia, he wrote to the officials of the thirteen states, introducing his ideas. By the time the delegates of the states met at the Constitutional **Convention** (also known as the Philadelphia Convention), in May 1787, Madison's plans for a federal Constitution were well known. The state of Virginia sent two delegates to the meeting: James Madison and George Washington.

George Washington at his Mount Vernon estate, where the ideas that led to the Constitution were debated.

The Philadelphia State House, where the Convention was held.

The Constitution is discussed

The Convention was held at the Philadelphia State House. It began on May 25, and George Washington was appointed the presiding officer. From the start, James Madison spoke convincingly about the need to replace the Articles of Confederation with a constitution—a set of rules that laid down the basis of the country's first national government. Through the summer of 1787, a total of 55 delegates from twelve of the thirteen states attended the Constitutional Convention. Only Rhode Island didn't attend, as it felt a strong federal government would end up taking power away from the states and leave them weaker.

Sign Here!

Some key principles were decided on at the beginning of the Constitutional Convention. The delegates agreed that voting should be by state, not by delegate. Also, they decided that the talks should be kept private while they were underway, so that delegates could speak openly. A public announcement would be made once they had reached a final agreement.

The Virginia Plan

On May 29, 1787, four days after the convention began, delegates began to discuss a draft constitution. It had been drafted mainly by James Madison, and because he represented Virginia, it came to be known as the "Virginia Plan." Madison proposed a system of federal government that had two houses, or chambers. Each house would be made up of representatives elected by voters from the thirteen states. The number of representatives elected would be based on how many people lived in the state.

The Virginia Plan was only a draft constitution, but it set the agenda for the debate yet to come.

William Paterson, author of the "New Jersey Plan."

The New Jersey Plan

Madison's Virginia Plan was hotly debated because not everyone was in favor of it. Delegates from states with small populations felt that it was unfair to them, since they would end up with fewer representatives than the larger states and might be outvoted. William Paterson, a delegate from New Jersey, proposed a different plan. Under the "New Jersey Plan," there would be one house of representatives, not two, and each state would have just one vote. The New Jersey Plan was rejected.

George Washington standing by the desk as the Constitution is signed.

The Great Compromise

At the beginning of July, after weeks of discussion, a Grand Committee was appointed to break the **deadlock**. After two weeks, the committee delivered its report. It was proposed that in the upper house (the Senate) each state should have an equal vote, regardless of how many people lived in the state. However, in the lower house (the House of Representatives) each state should have one representative for every 40,000 inhabitants. The Great Compromise, as it was called, was finally accepted on July 16, 1787.

The Great Compromise document brought together plans for a Senate and House of Representatives.

The Constitution is signed

In late July, delegates began drafting the final version of the Constitution. The Virginia Plan was the starting point, taking into account the recommendations of the Great Compromise. Even while the drafting and redrafting were going on, delegates continued to debate the text of the emerging Constitution. The question of slavery was fiercely argued; some states wanted it abolished, others did not. A compromise was reached that the slavery issue would be resolved at a future date.

After all the disagreements had been settled, the Constitution of the United States of America was signed on September 17, 1787. Of the 55 original delegates, 42 were present, and of those, 39 signed the historic document. Three delegates refused to sign; they believed the Constitution was flawed.

Key people in the painting:
1. George Washington, VA
2. Benjamin Franklin, PA
3. James Madison, VA
4. Alexander Hamilton, NY

We the People

"We the People of the United States, in Order to form a more perfect Union ..." So begins the Constitution of the United States, a landmark document not only for America, but for the entire Western world.

The Great Seal of the United States. It is used for documents issued by the US government to show they are genuine. The Great Seal was first used in 1782.

What is the Constitution?

The Constitution is the highest law in the United States. It sets out how the system of national government should work. Under the terms of the Constitution, the national government was divided into three branches—legislative, executive, and judicial.

Federal Government

The original hand-written Constitution of the United States of America.

Separation of power

It was important to separate the government's power among the three branches. It meant that no single branch had more power than the others, and each branch could watch over the others to make sure the system was working correctly.

Legislative branch

The day-to-day running of the government—the making of laws, the raising of money, and the power to declare war—was allocated to the legislative branch called Congress. It would be made up of the House of Representatives and the Senate.

Executive branch

At the head of the government there was to be a leader. He was given the title of "President." The president would be elected for a four-year term, and would be the commander-in-chief of the army and the navy. He could make treaties, appoint judges and diplomats, and his signature was needed before a new law could be passed.

Judicial branch

The Constitution created the Supreme Court to serve as the highest court in the country. Its job was to dispense justice.

Spreading the word

On September 19, 1787, two days after the Constitution was signed, the American people were given their first chance to read it. The Pennsylvania Packet and Daily Advertiser, printed in Philadelphia, became the first newspaper to print the full text of the Constitution. As more newspapers did the same, more people throughout the states were able to read the Constitution for themselves. It was also printed in pamphlets, and in the German language for German speakers in America.

The Pennsylvania Packet, and Daily Advertiser.

[Price Four-Pence.] WEDNESDAY, SEPTEMBER 19, 1787. [No. 2690.]

WE, the People of the United States, in order to form a more perfect Union, establish Justice, insure domestic Tranquility, provide for the common Defence, promote the General Welfare, and secure the Blessings of Liberty to Ourselves and our Posterity, do ordain and establish this Constitution for the United States of America.

The people of Pennsylvania were the first to read the full text of the Constitution when it was printed in a local newspaper.

Constitution at a glance

Number of words in 1787 document: 4,543, including the 39 signatures

Number of sheets: 4

Size of sheets: about 29 inches by 24 inches (74x61cm)

Written on: parchment (treated animal skin, probably sheepskin)

Written with: iron gall ink (made from oak galls and iron sulphate)

Reading time: takes about 30 minutes to read

Spelling mistakes: "Pensylvania" (for Pennsylvania), "it's" (for its), "chuse" (for choose, although "chuse" was acceptable at the time), and words spelled in the British manner: "defence" (for defense), and "labour" (for labor)

Where it is: National Archives, Washington, D.C.

James Madison, Father of the Constitution

Some years after the Constitution was **ratified** (agreed upon), James Madison became known as "The Father of the Constitution" because of all he had done to make it happen. He protested, saying it was "the work of many heads and many hands."

James Madison's birthplace at Port Conway, Virginia.

Early life

James Madison was born in 1751, on his grandparents' tobacco plantation at Port Conway, Virginia. He grew up in Orange County, Virginia, where his parents were prosperous tobacco planters. Madison was a gifted scholar. In 1769, he enrolled at the College of New Jersey (now Princeton University) where he completed a four-year course in two years. He studied history, languages, government or political science, and studied law with great interest.

Passion for politics

By 1774, Madison had focused on the biggest political issue at the time: independence from Great Britain, which he supported. In 1776, the year of the Declaration of Independence, Madison helped draft the Virginia Constitution. The colony declared its freedom from British rule and created the Virginia Assembly to govern its own affairs. The Virginia Constitution was important not only for Virginia, but for the future of the United States, because it showed what was possible for the other colonies. It also shaped James Madison's personal future.

Man of ideas

Between May and September 1787, Madison addressed delegates many times at the Constitutional Convention, held in Philadelphia. He spoke clearly and convincingly about his ideas for a national government. Madison believed the United States needed a strong central government in which power was divided into three branches so that none could overrule the others. Delegates agreed with Madison, and his ideas became part of the Constitution of the United States of America.

His work did not end there, as the Constitution had to be ratified, or approved, by the states. To advocate ratification, Madison, with help from supporters, won approval for the Constitution by writing a series of articles for newspapers.

James Madison addressing the Constitutional Convention.

General Andrew Jackson at the battle of New Orleans.

Fourth President

James Madison served as the fourth President of the United States (1809–1817). In 1812, a group of politicians urged him to declare war on Great Britain because the British had seized American ships and sailors. Madison was reluctant to send the new nation to war, but he did. The War of 1812 ended in 1815, with neither side able to claim an outright victory. However, it brought the states closer together, and the US emerged as a stronger nation.

Final years

Madison left office in 1817, and spent the rest of his life on his 5,000-acre tobacco plantation at Montpelier, Orange County, Virginia. He believed in modern methods of farming without the exploitation of slaves, worked to abolish slavery, and helped to resettle freed slaves in Liberia, West Africa. He died in 1836, aged 85.

"Every person seems to acknowledge his greatness. In the management of every great question he evidently took the lead in the Convention."

—William Pierce, describing James Madison at the Constitutional Convention

Ratifying the Constitution

The Constitution, which was signed on September 17, 1787, at the Constitutional Convention, did not come into force immediately. It had to be ratified, or approved, by at least nine of the thirteen states.

The states debate

A few days after the Constitution was signed, Congress sent printed copies of it to all thirteen states. Each state held a meeting to discuss it. This was the first chance for American citizens to talk about the plans for a new government. Five state conventions voted to approve the Constitution almost immediately (Delaware, Pennsylvania, New Jersey, Georgia, Connecticut). Other states were less certain, and very soon a split had opened up between those in favor and those not in favor of the Constitution. The future of the fledgling United States was in the hands of the American people.

Federalists: in favor

People who supported the Constitution called themselves "Federalists." Many were rich businesspeople, such as property owners, planters, and merchants, and professional people, including lawyers. Supporters tended to live in towns, not in the countryside. The Federalist cause was helped because the two most famous men in America—Benjamin Franklin (above, Pennsylvania) and George Washington (Virginia)—supported it. Also, because most newspapers were owned by Federalists, they printed articles (the "Federalist Papers") in favor of the Constitution.

Anti-Federalists: not in favor

People opposed to the Constitution were called "Anti-Federalists." Their greatest fear was that individual states would have power taken from them by a national government, leaving them weaker than before. Anti-Federalists tended to live in the countryside, where they worked on small farms. Like the Federalists, they also had influential men on their side. Patrick Henry (above) and Richard Henry Lee (Virginia), Jam Winthrop (Massachusetts), and George Clinton (New York) all criticized the Constitution.

THE

FEDERALIST:

ADDRESSED TO THE

PEOPLE OF THE STATE OF NEW-YORK.

NUMBER I.

Introduction.

AFTER an unequivocal experience of the ineffi-cacy of the subsisting federal government, you are called upon to deliberate on a new constitution for the United States of America. The subject speaks its own importance; comprehending in its consequences, nothing less than the existence of the UNION, the safety and welfare of the parts of which it is composed, the fate of an empire, in many respects, the most interesting in the world. It has been frequently remarked, that it seems to have been reserved to the people of this country, by their conduct and example, to decide the important question, whether societies of men are really capable or not, of establishing good government from reflection and choice, or whether they are forever destined to depend, for their political constitutions, on accident and force. If there be any truth in the remark, the crisis, at which we are arrived, may with propriety be regarded as the æra in which

that

Federalist Papers

In an effort to persuade voters to approve the Constitution, Federalists James Madison (Virginia), Alexander Hamilton, and John Jay (New York) used newspapers to spread their message. Between 1787 and 1788 they wrote 85 essays that explained what it would mean to have a national government. Most of these "Federalist Papers" were first printed in New York state newspapers, after which they were printed in newspapers in other states. The essays convinced people to vote in favor of the Constitution. The identity of the three authors (Madison, Hamilton, and Jay) was a closely guarded secret, and instead of using their own names, each essay was attributed to the made-up author "Publius."

The Federalist Papers helped to promote the Constitution as a good idea for the people of America.

Ratification of the Constitution

STATE	DATE OF ENTRY INTO THE UNION
1. Delaware	December 7, 1787
2. Pennsylvania	December 12, 1787
3. New Jersey	December 18, 1787
4. Georgia	January 2, 1788
5. Connecticut	January 9, 1788
6. Massachusetts	February 6, 1788
7. Maryland	April 28, 1788
8. South Carolina	May 23, 1788
9. New Hampshire	June 21, 1788
10. Virginia	June 26, 1788
11. New York	July 26, 1788
12. North Carolina	November 21, 1789
13. Rhode Island	May 29, 1790

Political cartoon showing the states as a series of pillars. The message was "united they stand, divided they fall."

"A more perfect Union"

By June 21, 1788, nine of the thirteen states had voted to ratify the Constitution. On that day, the opening words of the Constitution, "We the people, in order to form a more perfect Union," had become true. By late May 1790, the remaining four states had also voted in favor.

George Washington, First President

Six months after the Constitution was ratified, the process of electing the first president of the United States began. The election was held over 27 days, from December 15, 1788, to January 10, 1789.

How should a president be addressed? It was soon decided that President Washington should be greeted as "Mr. President." It set the style that is used to this day.

Only one candidate

Unlike a modern-day presidential election, in which there are several **candidates** to choose from, the election of 1789 had only one candidate: George Washington, the hero of the American Revolutionary War. He had presided over the 1787 Constitutional Convention, had signed the Constitution, and he had helped in the lengthy process of ratifying it. With that work over, Washington had hoped to **retire** to his Mount Vernon farm in Virginia. But his role in the forming of the country had been so important that all eyes were on him to become the nation's first president. As expected, Washington "won" the election.

Inauguration

After he was elected, Washington traveled from Mount Vernon to New York, and along the way people came out to greet him. He crossed the Hudson River in a specially built barge decorated in red, white, and blue, then made his way to Federal Hall on Wall Street in New York. There, on April 30, 1789, he stood on the balcony and was sworn in, or **inaugurated**, as the first President of the United States of America.

George Washington arrives in New York on board a barge. It was rowed by thirteen men, and ships fired thirteen-gun salutes.

> "He was, indeed, in every sense of the words, a wise, a good, and a great man."
>
> —Thomas Jefferson, describing George Washington

Whiskey rebellion

The first real test for the new government came in 1794, when farmers in Pennsylvania began a rebellion. They were unhappy about having to pay a new tax on alcohol, and when government officials tried to collect the money, the farmers attacked them. After President Washington ordered 13,000 troops into the area from neighboring states, the farmers withdrew and the rebellion came to an end. It showed the power of the national government and the authority of the president as leader of the nation.

Lasting legacy

George Washington proved to be an excellent first president. His presidential powers were laid out in the Constitution, and he followed them carefully. By doing this he set a good example for all later presidents to follow, and earned respect for the United States from world powers such as Great Britain, France, and Spain. In 1791, he helped choose a site for the nation's new capital. The city was to be built along the Potomac River, and was named Washington in his honor.

A tax collector is covered in sticky tar and feathers by farmers opposed to the tax on alcohol.

Final years

Washington was such a popular president that some people wanted him to carry on forever—but he couldn't. The Constitution fixed a president's term of office at four years. Washington's first term came to an end in 1792, and in the election that followed he was reelected for a second term. He refused to stand for a third term, and retired in 1797. His last years were spent at his Mount Vernon home, where he died in 1799.

George Washington's tomb, at his home at Mount Vernon.

Political Parties Emerge

All governments have people with strong views, and during George Washington's presidency this was no different. Toward the end of his first term, two of his most senior officials disagreed over how the government should work. As the difference of opinion grew, the first political parties emerged: the Federalists and the Democratic-Republicans.

Alexander Hamilton

Thomas Jefferson

An old argument

Washington was disappointed that Alexander Hamilton and Thomas Jefferson disagreed so strongly. Their argument was getting more heated, and the issue wasn't going away. In fact, it had been around for a long time, and now was splitting the government in two. The question of how much power the government should have had already been raised at the drafting of the Constitution and during its ratification, and yet it was still not resolved. When Washington gave his Farewell Address in 1796, at the end of his second term, he warned against the creation of "political **factions**," but by then it was too late to change the course of history.

The Federalist Party

Alexander Hamilton became the leader of the Federalist Party, which was formed in 1791. Hamilton believed in a strong and powerful national government, led by talented, well-educated people. Federalists believed the government should:

- **take responsibility for the** debt **from the Revolutionary War;**

- **raise money through taxes;**

- **create a central bank; and**

- **give favorable treatment to American shipping and merchants.**

The Democratic-Republican Party

Thomas Jefferson became the leader of the Democratic-Republican Party. It was formed in 1792, as an opposition party to the Federalists. Jefferson was opposed to an all-powerful national government. His greatest fear was that ordinary Americans would lose their **liberty**—that they would not be listened to. Republicans, as they were known, believed:

- **national government had too much power;**

- **the president could start to act like a king or a dictator;**

- **a Federalist government favored the rich at the expense of the poor; and**

- **education was the key to improving people's lives.**

THE PROVIDENTIAL DETECTION

A political cartoon attacking Thomas Jefferson. It shows him kneeling before an altar, on top of which a fire burns. Jefferson is about to throw the US Constitution onto the fire, but he's stopped from doing so by an American eagle.

Alexander Hamilton, Government Official

Alexander Hamilton rose from a humble background to become one of the Founding Fathers of the United States. He helped to draft the Constitution, became the first Secretary of the Treasury, and laid the foundations for a strong economy.

Early life

Hamilton was born in 1757 on Nevis, a small island in the Caribbean Sea that belonged to Britain. He had a talent for mathematics, and in particular, for bookkeeping—keeping an accurate record of the money passing through a business. For a time, while still in his teens, he was the manager of a trading company. Then, aged 15, he was sent to study in America.

Nevis, the birthplace of Alexander Hamilton.

Getting into politics

Hamilton arrived in America in 1772, just at the time when people were talking about breaking away from Great Britain. He was in support of America's freedom, and described his ideas in pamphlets that were widely read. During the American Revolutionary War, Hamilton served as one of General George Washington's most senior **advisors**. After the war, he became a spokesman for the state of New York. He was in favor of a strong national government, and was one of the 39 delegates who signed the Constitution in 1787. By writing articles as part of the "Federalist Papers," Hamilton helped win support for the Constitution during its ratification process.

The *New York Evening Post* was a Federalist newspaper founded by Alexander Hamilton in 1801.

Alexander Hamilton's portrait is used on the front of the current US $10 bill.

Secretary of the Treasury

In 1789, President Washington appointed Hamilton the first Secretary of the Treasury. His job was to deal with the finances of the new nation. He wanted to raise money through taxation, which would pay off the debts of the American Revolutionary War. He wanted the government to create a central bank and give help to American businesses. These were bold ideas that Hamilton believed would make a strong national government. Yet they went too far for some politicians. A split appeared in Washington's government, out of which emerged America's first political parties: the Federalists, led by Hamilton, and the Democratic-Republicans, led by Thomas Jefferson.

The duel between Alexander Hamilton (right) and Aaron Burr (left).

Duel to the death

Hamilton's number-one political enemy was Aaron Burr, then Vice President of the United States, from the state of New York. The men had clashed in debates several times, but things boiled over in 1804. Hamilton stated that Burr was not to be trusted with the reins of government, and in response Burr challenged Hamilton to a **duel**. The pair faced each other at dawn on July 11, 1804, at Weehawken, New Jersey. Pistol shots rang out. Hamilton's bullet snapped a branch above Burr's head; the bullet from Burr's pistol struck Hamilton's body. Hamilton died the next day.

Building the Capital

Every nation has a capital city. The capital of the United States of America is Washington, D.C., named after George Washington, its first president.

Washington was laid out on a grid pattern of streets. The city plan was designed by Pierre Charles L'Enfant, and was known as the "L'Enfant Plan."

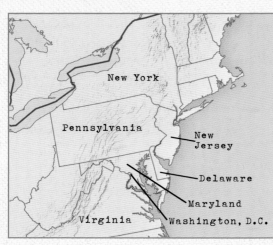

Pierre Charles L'Enfant (1754-1825)

Choosing the site

On July 9, 1790, Congress passed the Residence Act, which approved the creation of a national capital on the Potomac River. It was to be built in what was then the middle of the country, as the thirteen original states ran along the eastern coastline. Maryland and Virginia had donated land for the capital, and to avoid either state claiming that Washington was within their state boundaries, the capital was given its own territory, named the District of Columbia (as a reference to the explorer Christopher Columbus).

Marking the boundaries

The city was to be built in a square, with 10-mile-long (16-km-long) sides. The key buildings of the government would be built within its borders. Before anything could be built, the land had to be surveyed. A team of **surveyors** marked out the boundaries of the new capital, placing sandstone boundary markers every mile (1.6km) along the sides of the square.

Planning the city

In early 1791, President Washington appointed Pierre Charles L'Enfant, a civil engineer, to draw up a plan for the capital. Born in France, L'Enfant had moved to America in his twenties. In the "L'Enfant Plan," Washington was to have a grassy m running through its center. On either side would be rectangular city blocks, with wi avenues. Among the key buildings would the President's House (the White House), and a building for the government to mee in (the Capitol).

> "I pray Heaven to bestow the best of blessings on this house and all that shall hereafter inhabit it. May none but honest and wise men ever rule under this roof."

—President John Adams, on his first night in the White House, November 1, 1800

The White House

James Hoban, an Irish architect living in Philadelphia, Pennsylvania, won the competition to design the president's home. President Washington took great interest in the design, and insisted that it was faced with sandstone. The first stone was laid in 1792, and after eight years of building, President John Adams, America's second president, became the first president to live there. Because the outside of the building was painted white, it wasn't long before it became known as the "White House."

The Capitol

The winning design for the government headquarters came from William Thornton. He had studied medicine in Scotland before moving to America, where he worked as an architect. The foundation stone for the Capitol was laid in 1793. Very slowly the building began to rise until, in 1800, it was used for the first meeting of Congress. Construction work continued and changes were made to the design. One of the biggest changes came in 1855, when work began to build the huge dome that is known the world over today.

The United States Capitol, on Capitol Hill, Washington, D.C., is where Congress meets.

Washington burns!

On August 24, 1814, British troops occupied Washington, D.C. during the War of 1812. They had orders to burn public buildings, and both the White House and the Capitol were set on fire and were badly damaged. The British withdrew from the city the next day.

Destruction of Washington, D.C. by the British in the War of 1812. In the distance the White House can be seen burning.

29

Amending the Constitution

James Madison addressing the Virginia Constitutional Convention at Richmond, 1829. Madison, who was then aged almos[t] 80, spoke against giving slaves in Virginia the right to vote.

It can be very difficult to get a group of people to all agree to the same thing. This is just what happened during the ratification, or approval, process, when the thirteen original states discussed the Constitution. Some states argued that it needed changing, while other states were satisfied with it as it was.

A "living document"

The Constitution has been called a "living document" or a "work in progress." It's a way of saying that it can be changed, so it lives and grows as America changes through time. Right from the start, there were calls for change. During the ratification process, more than 200 changes to the Constitution were proposed by the states. James Madison reviewed them all. He took out all those proposals that he and President Washington thought were against the interests of the new national government. Madison was left with a list of twelve changes, or **amendments**, called for by the states.

The Constitution was handwritten by Jacob Shallus of Pennsylvania, who was paid $30 for his work.

Bill of Rights

On December 15, 1791, the states agreed to ten of the twelve amendments on Madison's list (two were rejected). The amendments were added to the Constitution, and are known as the Bill of Rights. They are designed t[o] protect the rights of individual American peopl[e] and place limits on the power of both national and state governments.

The Bill of Rights of 1791 did not apply to all Americans, as it was designed to protect land-owning white men only. Black people, Native Americans, and women had to fight for equal rights. Their struggle for equality continued for the following 130 years.

> "I wish the plan was prefaced with a Bill of Rights. And I would second a motion if made for the purpose. It would give great quiet to the people."
>
> —George Mason, Virginia delegate to the Constitutional Convention

A commemorative five-dollar gold coin featuring James Madison and the Bill of Rights.

The first ten amendments

First amendment

All US citizens have the right to freedom of speech, to practice their chosen religion, and to protest peacefully.

Second amendment

All US citizens have the right to carry a weapon for self-defense.

Third amendment

All US citizens have the right to refuse soldiers from occupying their home, except if there is a war on.

Fourth amendment

All US citizens have the right to refuse being searched, or having their home searched, unless a judge believes a crime has been committed.

Fifth amendment

All US citizens have the right to a fair trial, and cannot be tried for the same crime twice.

Sixth amendment

All US citizens have the right to a public trial, a lawyer to assist them, to know what they are accused of, and a jury of ordinary citizens from their own area.

Seventh amendment

All US citizens have the right to a jury in a civil case (a law case between two people).

Eighth amendment

All US citizens have the right to a fair and reasonable punishment if convicted of a crime.

Ninth amendment

All US citizens have the right to other rights that are not listed in the Constitution.

Tenth amendment

Rights that are not covered by the Constitution can be made by the individual states or the people.

The Nation Grows

"New States may be admitted
by the Congress into this Unio[n]
—Constitution, Article IV

How big was the new nation of the United States? Everyone knew there were thirteen states, but how many people lived in them? The only way to find out was to count them all.

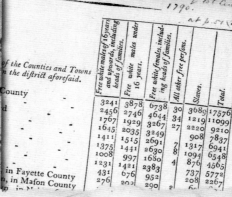

An image of New York Harbor teeming with boats in 1830.

First census

On Monday, August 2, 1790, a little more than a year after the inauguration of President George Washington, the nation's first **census** was held (a census has been held every ten years since then). Marshals visited every household in every state. They gathered information about the head of the family, and the number of people living in each household according to the following descriptions:

- **free white males aged 16 years and upward;**
- **free white males aged under 16 years;**
- **free white females;**
- **all other free persons; and**
- **slaves.**

Native North Americans were not counted in the 1790 census.

The first census figures for Kentucky, 1790. The census recorded 73,677 people living in the state.

How many people?

When all the figures were in, the number of people in the thirteen states was found to be just under four million —3,929,214, to be exact.

Biggest cities in 1790

City	Population
1 New York City, NY	33,131
2 Philadelphia, PA	28,522
3 Boston, MA	18,320
4 Charleston, SC	16,359
5 Baltimore, MD	13,503

New states admitted to the Union

The Constitution allows for the creation of new states, and on March 4, 1791, Vermont became the nation's fourteenth state, followed a few years later by Kentucky (15th, 1792) and Tennessee (sixteenth, 1796). The nineteenth century saw the admittance of twenty-nine states, and five more were admitted during the twentieth century. As each new state joined the Union, the nation grew in size.

Western borders were still evolving when this map was made in 1866.

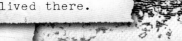

The 1790 census for the state of New York showed that 340,120 people lived there.

Star-Spangled Banner

Every nation needs a flag, and the first US flag was created in 1776. It had thirteen alternating red and white stripes and thirteen white stars on a blue background—one stripe and one star for each of the thirteen original states. As new states have been admitted to the Union, the flag has been changed many times.

Flag of 1776
(13 stars)

Texas flag, 19th century
(15 stars)

Flag of the Battle of Bennington, 1777
(13 stars)

Flag of 1959
(49 stars)

Flag of 1781
(13 stars)

Flag of 1960
(50 stars)

John Adams, Second President

As one of the nation's Founding Fathers, John Adams helped draft the Declaration of Independence. He was a diplomat, served as President George Washington's vice president, and he became the nation's second president in 1797.

Gifted diplomat

Adams was born in 1735, in Braintree (now Quincy), Massachusetts. He became a successful lawyer in Boston, and when Great Britain increased the tax paid by her American colonies, Adams spoke out against it. He was a leading delegate at the First and Second Continental Congresses (1774 and 1775), where he called for America to break away from Britain. During the American Revolutionary War, he was a **diplomat** in both France and Holland. After the war, he led the American delegation to Paris, where the peace treaty was signed.

"The most insignificant office"

In 1789, Adams became vice president under President George Washington. He was America's first vice president. Adams soon discovered that the vice president had no real power, and described the job as "the most insignificant office." He found it a frustrating experience, but he did his duty until 1797.

USS *Constitution* was launched in 1797. She was armed with 44 guns and served with distinction with the US Navy. In the War of 1812, fought against Britain, she captured several British merchant ships and defeated five warships.

Father of the navy

After eight years as vice president, Adams became the nation's second president in 1797. Immediately, he had to deal with an international crisis. Britain and France were at war, and French warships were attacking US ships to prevent them from trading with Britain. President Adams ordered warships to be built, which became the first ships in the US Navy. They sank several French ships until, in 1800, Adams brought an end to the conflict. The same year, Adams and his family moved to their new home: the White House, Washington, D.C. He was the first president to live there.

Abigail Adams (1744-1818)

Abigail Adams, First Lady

Abigail and John Adams were married in 1764. She ran the family farm, brought up their children (one of whom, John Quincy Adams, became the nation's sixth president), and took care of her husband's business affairs. She was interested in politics, and held strong opinions on many political issues. For example, she was against slavery, and she believed that everyone had the right to a good education.

"It ought to be solemnized with pomp and parade, with shows, games, sports, guns, bells, bonfires, and illuminations, from one end of this continent to the other, from this time forward, forever more."

—John Adams, describing his idea to celebrate July 4th, Independence Day

This stamp featuring President John Adams was issued in 1938.

Final years

Adams hoped to be reelected as president for a second term. But during the election, held in 1800, he was defeated by his rival, Thomas Jefferson. Adams retired to his family farm, where he died in 1826.

Alien and Sedition Acts

King Louis XIV of France being led to the guillotine during the French Revolution.

In 1798, President Adams's Federalist government passed four laws designed to strengthen the security of the new nation. They were called the **Alien** and **Sedition** Acts. Although they were popular with most people, they raised questions about how much power the national government should have.

First security crisis

When John Adams became president in 1797, he faced the prospect of a war with France. French ships had attacked US merchant ships, and it looked as if the two nations were heading toward conflict. It was the first security crisis faced by the government— and something had to be done.

Dangerous strangers

At the same time as the French attacks on US ships, there was great unrest in France because the French Revolution was in full swing. People lived in fear of losing their lives, and many fled from France to the US, where they hoped to start afresh. However, the US government saw a problem with this. What if these "political refugees" (this is how they would be described today) brought along ideas of starting a similar revolution in America? That would pose a danger to the US government.

FIFTH CONGRESS OF THE UNITED STATES:

At the Second Session.

Begun and held at the city of *Philadelphia*, in the state of PENNSYLVANIA, on *Monday*, the thirteenth of *November*, one thousand seven hundred and ninety-seven.

An ACT concerning aliens.

The text of the Alien Act. It came into law in case the US went to war with France.

Clampdown on foreigners

In June and July 1798, the government passed three laws, known as the Alien Acts ("alien" means "foreigner"). The new laws gave the US government the following powers:

- **the power to detain a person from an enemy nation;**

- **the power to expel a foreign person, if the government thought the person was a danger to the US; and**

- **the power to make it harder for a foreign person to become a US citizen.**

Clampdown on the press

In July 1798, the government passed the Sedition Act ("sedition" means "encouraging people to rebel against the state"). It became illegal to publish anything that criticized the government or its president. The Sedition Act was a clampdown on the freedom of the press.

Good or bad laws?

The Alien and Sedition Acts were precautions. They were security measures designed to protect the government and the people of the United States from threats that could lead to unrest, and worse, a revolution. The new laws were popular among ordinary Americans, but Thomas Jefferson and his supporters in the Republican Party were against them, believing that they gave too much power to the national government.

Attack on the president

Soon after the Sedition Act became law, Matthew Lyon, a politician from Vermont, wrote a newspaper article that attacked President Adams. Not only did Lyon accuse the president of acting like a king (a way of saying he had too much power), but he said that President Adams should be sent to a "madhouse." Lyon was put on trial and found guilty of sedition. He was sentenced to four months in prison.

End of the laws

America and France did not go to war, and in 1800 Jefferson and the Republican Party were elected to power. Over the next two years, the Alien and Sedition Acts were abolished. In the short time they had been in force, only one foreigner was deported and only ten people were convicted for sedition.

Thomas Jefferson, Third President

Thomas Jefferson's skill with words was unrivaled, which led to him being chosen to draft the Declaration of Independence. He was leader of the Republican Party, and in 1801 he became America's third president.

Early life

Jefferson was born in 1743, in Shadwell, Virginia. A gifted student, he would spend 15 hours a day studying his books, and three hours a day practicing the violin. He became a lawyer, and that meant he had to speak in public—something he didn't enjoy. He came across as shy and nervous, which could have been seen as a weakness. Instead, his formidable legal skills shone through.

"A Summary View of the Rights of British America" was written by Thomas Jefferson in 1774. In it, Jefferson said that America should be independent from Britain.

Draftsman of the Declaration of Independence

In 1768, Jefferson was elected to a group of leading officials, called the Virginia House of Burgesses. Six years later he wrote a pamphlet calling for America's independence from Great Britain. He became noticed, and the following year, 1775, he was made a delegate for Virginia at the Second Continental Congress. Jefferson said very little during the debates—his shyness got the better of him. Instead, his role was to listen to what was said, then write what had been agreed, clearly and correctly. In 1776, Jefferson was given the task of drafting the Declaration of Independence. He put into words what many Americans already believed: that America was right to break away from Britain.

"Educate and inform the who mass of the people. They are the only sure reliance for the preservation of our liberty."

—Thomas Jefferson, describing the importance of education

Party leader

Toward the end of President George Washington's first term in office, two political parties emerged. They had opposing ideas about how the national government should run the country. Jefferson was leader of the Democratic-Republican Party, or Republicans. Its members believed the government should have limited powers, and should not control ordinary Americans too much.

President Jefferson

Jefferson served as vice president under President John Adams. When the two became rivals in the election of 1800, Jefferson emerged as the winner. He was America's first Republican president, and was well liked by the people. Among his many achievements, he cut taxes and saved money by reducing the size of the army and navy. In 1803, Jefferson doubled the size of the US when he purchased the Louisiana Territory from France.

Cartoon showing President Jefferson addressing a group of American merchants, who are unhappy at what he is saying. The president is defending his embargo on trading with Britain.

Second-term difficulties

In 1804, Jefferson was reelected to serve for a second time as president. This was the time of the Napoleonic Wars, mainly fought between Great Britain and France. Jefferson tried to avoid taking sides and keep America out of the conflict. He thought it was a good idea to embargo (stop) British and French goods from entering the United States. But his plan backfired, American trade suffered, and he became an unpopular president.

Jefferson's home at Monticello, Virginia.

Final years

Jefferson left office in 1809, and retired to his family home at Monticello, Virginia. He wrote thousands of letters, important visitors came to see him, and he began establishing the University of Virginia. He died in 1826.

The Louisiana Purchase

"The object of your mission is to explore the Missouri River and communicate with the waters of the Pacific Ocean for the purposes of commerce."

—Thomas Jefferson's instructions to Lewis and Clark

Since its break from Great Britain in 1776, the US had grown slowly. By 1803, there were sixteen unrivaled states in the Union, located on the eastern side of North America. That year the young nation increased in size when President Thomas Jefferson bought a vast area of land.

Port of New Orleans

When Jefferson became president in 1801, one of his top priorities was to purchase the port of New Orleans. At that time, New Orleans belonged to France—but Jefferson wanted it for the US. It lay in a prime location at the mouth of the Mississippi River, on the Gulf of Mexico. If Jefferson could buy New Orleans from the French, it would mean good business for American farmers and merchants, who would be able to use the port to ship goods in and out of the country—without having to pay tax.

New Orleans, as the city appeared in about 1851.

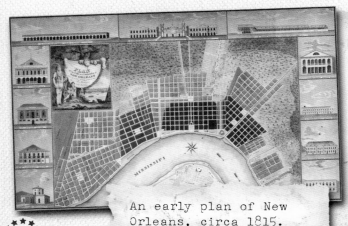

An early plan of New Orleans, circa 1815.

Greatest land bargain in US history

The US offered France $2 million for New Orleans. France rejected the offer; it was not enough. In 1803, the US increased its offer to $10 million. This time, France accepted. However, France said that for an additional $5 million the US could also have Louisiana. This was the name France had given to the vast lands it controlled from the Mississippi River in the east to the Rocky Mountains in the west, and from the Gulf of Mexico in the south to the Canadian border in the north. It was named Louisiana for the French king, Louis XIV (14th). For $15 million, Jefferson's Louisiana Purchase amounted to 828,000 square miles (2.15 million km/sq) of land. This worked out at about three cents an acre—an incredible bargain.

New states created

In time, the new territory was divided into the states of Louisiana, Missouri, Arkansas, Iowa, North Dakota, South Dakota, Nebraska, Kansas, Colorado, Wyoming, Montana, Minnesota, and Oklahoma. The Louisiana Purchase, as it was known, doubled the size of the United States, and set the scene for the nation's westward expansion.

The territory of the Louisiana Purchase (in green).

Mapping the nation

Jefferson was curious to find out what lay to the west of the nation. Shortly after the Louisiana Purchase, he set Meriwether Lewis and William Clark the task of finding out. For two years, 1804–1806, Lewis and Clark led an expedition westward as far as the Pacific coast, charting the vast, unknown region. The Lewis and Clark expedition covered about 8,000 miles (nearly 13,000km) and discovered 178 new plants and 122 species of animals. It was a remarkable achievement. The expedition mapped the nation for the first time, filling in the western side of the map as far as the Pacific Ocean.

Discovering the Legacy of Lewis and Clark
BICENTENNIAL COMMEMORATION 2003–2006

Route taken by the Lewis and Clark expedition westward across the US (red).

Meriwether Lewis

William Clark

Legacy of the Founding Fathers

Throughout the 1800s, settlers moved west. They came from the existing states in the east of the country, and from overseas—particularly from countries in central Europe and Scandinavia. New states were created, and by 1900 the US was a nation of 45 states with a population of 76 million. In a little over 125 years, the nation had grown from a small group of colonies into an independent country with a strong government and a written constitution. It was what the country's founders had worked hard to achieve—for the benefit of future generations.

The Founding Fathers

Twelve of the thirteen original states sent delegates to the Constitutional Convention, held in Philadelphia in 1787. Only Rhode Island stayed away. Of the 55 delegates, 39 signed the historic Constitution document, 13 left the meeting early and did not sign, and three refused to sign.

New Hampshire

Founding Father: Nicholas Gilman
Constitution document: Signed
Born–Died: 1755–1814
Occupation: Politician, merchant

Founding Father: John Langdon
Constitution document: Signed
Born–Died: 1741–1819
Occupation: Politician, merchant

Connecticut

Founding Father: Oliver Ellsworth
Constitution document: Did not sign (left early)
Born–Died: 1745–1807
Occupation: Politician, lawyer

Founding Father: William Johnson
Constitution document: Signed
Born–Died: 1727–1819
Occupation: Politician, clergyman

Founding Father: Roger Sherman
Constitution document: Signed
Born–Died: 1721–1793
Occupation: Politician, lawyer

Massachusetts

Founding Father: Elbridge Gerry
Constitution document: Refused to sign
Born–Died: 1744–1814
Occupation: Politician

Founding Father: Nathaniel Gorham
Constitution document: Signed
Born–Died: 1738–1796
Occupation: Politician, merchant

Founding Father: Rufus King
Constitution document: Signed
Born–Died: 1755–1827
Occupation: Politician, lawyer, diplomat

Founding Father: Caleb Strong
Constitution document: Did not sign (left early)
Born–Died: 1745–1819
Occupation: Politician, lawyer

Delaware

Founding Father: Richard Bassett
Constitution document: Signed
Born–Died: 1745–1815
Occupation: Politician, lawyer

Founding Father: Gunning Bedford, Jr.
Constitution document: Signed
Born–Died: 1747–1812
Occupation: Politician, lawyer

Founding Father: Jacob Broom
Constitution document: Signed
Born–Died: 1752–1810
Occupation: Politician, businessman

Founding Father: John Dickinson
Constitution document: Signed
Born–Died: 1732–1808
Occupation: Politician, lawyer

Founding Father: George Read
Constitution document: Signed
Born–Died: 1733–1798
Occupation: Politician, lawyer

Georgia

Founding Father: Abraham Baldwin
Constitution document: Signed
Born–Died: 1754–1807
Occupation: Politician

Founding Father: William Few
Constitution document: Signed
Born–Died: 1748–1828
Occupation: Politician, businessman, farmer

Founding Father: William Houston
Constitution document: Did not sign (left early)
Born–Died: ca. 1755–1813
Occupation: Politician, lawyer, planter

Founding Father: William L. Pierce
Constitution document: Did not sign (left early)
Born–Died: ca. 1753–1789
Occupation: Politician, merchant

Maryland

Founding Father: Daniel Carroll
Constitution document: Signed
Born–Died: 1730–1796
Occupation: Politician, planter

Founding Father: James McHenry
Constitution document: Signed
Born–Died: 1753–1816
Occupation: Politician, surgeon

Founding Father: Luther Martin
Constitution document: Did not sign (left early)
Born–Died: 1748–1826
Occupation: Politician, lawyer

Founding Father: John F. Mercer
Constitution document: Did not sign (left early)
Born–Died: 1759–1821
Occupation: Politician, lawyer, planter

Founding Father: Daniel St. Thomas Jenifer
Constitution document: Signed
Born–Died: 1723–1790
Occupation: Politician, planter

New Jersey

Founding Father: David Brearly
Constitution document: Signed
Born–Died: 1745–1790
Occupation: Politician, lawyer

Founding Father: Jonathan Dayton
Constitution document: Signed
Born–Died: 1760–1824
Occupation: Politician, lawyer

Founding Father: William C. Houston
Constitution document: Did not sign
(left early)
Born–Died: ca. 1746–1788
Occupation: Politician, teacher

Founding Father: William Livingston
Constitution document: Signed
Born–Died: 1723–1790
Occupation: Politician, lawyer

Founding Father: William Paterson
Constitution document: Signed
Born–Died: 1745–1806
Occupation: Politician, lawyer

New York

Founding Father: Alexander Hamilton
Constitution document: Signed
Born–Died: 1755–1804
Occupation: Politician, lawyer

Founding Father: John Lansing, Jr.
Constitution document: Did not sign
(left early)
Born–Died: 1754–1829
Occupation: Politician, lawyer

Founding Father: Robert Yates
Constitution document: Did not sign
(left early)
Born–Died: 1738–1801
Occupation: Politician, judge

North Carolina

Founding Father: William Blount
Constitution document: Signed
Born–Died: 1749–1800
Occupation: Politician

Founding Father: William R. Davie
Constitution document: Did not sign
(left early)
Born–Died: 1756–1820
Occupation: Politician, lawyer

Founding Father: Alexander Martin
Constitution document: Did not sign
(left early)
Born–Died: 1740–1807
Occupation: Politician, judge

Founding Father: Richard D. Spaight
Constitution document: Signed
Born–Died: 1758–1802
Occupation: Politician, lawyer

Founding Father: Hugh Williamson
Constitution document: Signed
Born–Died: 1735–1819
Occupation: Politician, doctor

South Carolina

Founding Father: Pierce Butler
Constitution document: Signed
Born–Died: 1744–1822
Occupation: Politician, soldier, planter

Founding Father: Charles Pinckney
Constitution document: Signed
Born–Died: 1757–1824
Occupation: Politician, lawyer

Founding Father: Charles Cotesworth Pinckney
Constitution document: Signed
Born–Died: 1746–1825
Occupation: Politician, lawyer, planter, soldier

Founding Father: John Rutledge
Constitution document: Signed
Born–Died: 1739–1800
Occupation: Politician, judge

Pennsylvania

Founding Father: George Clymer
Constitution document: Signed
Born–Died: 1739–1813
Occupation: Politician, merchant

Founding Father: Thomas Fitzsimons
Constitution document: Signed
Born–Died: 1741–1811
Occupation: Politician, merchant

Founding Father: Benjamin Franklin
Constitution document: Signed
Born–Died: 1706–1790
Occupation: Politician, printer, publisher, scientist, diplomat

Founding Father: Jared Ingersoll
Constitution document: Signed
Born–Died: 1749–1822
Occupation: Politician, lawyer

Founding Father: Thomas Mifflin
Constitution document: Signed
Born–Died: 1744–1800
Occupation: Politician, merchant

Founding Father: Gouverneur Morris
Constitution document: Signed
Born–Died: 1752–1816
Occupation: Politician, lawyer

Founding Father: Robert Morris
Constitution document: Signed
Born–Died: 1734–1806
Occupation: Politician, banker

Founding Father: James Wilson
Constitution document: Signed
Born–Died: 1742–1798
Occupation: Politician, lawyer

Virginia

Founding Father: John Blair
Constitution document: Signed
Born–Died: 1732–1800
Occupation: Politician, lawyer

Founding Father: James Madison, Jr.
Constitution document: Signed
Born–Died: 1751–1836
Occupation: Politician

Founding Father: George Mason
Constitution document: Refused to sign
Born–Died: 1725–1792
Occupation: Politician, planter

Founding Father: James McClurg
Constitution document: Did not sign (left early)
Born–Died: 1746–1823
Occupation: Politician, surgeon, doctor

Founding Father: Edmund J. Randolph
Constitution document: Refused to sign
Born–Died: 1753–1813
Occupation: Politician, lawyer

Founding Father: George Washington
Constitution document: Signed
Born–Died: 1732–1799
Occupation: Politician, soldier

Founding Father: George Wythe
Constitution document: Did not sign (left early)
Born–Died: 1726–1806
Occupation: Politician, lawyer

GLOSSARY

ADVISOR
A person who gives advice to someone.

ALIEN
A person from another country.

AMBASSADOR
An official person sent as a representative by their country to another country.

AMENDMENT
A change or alteration to something.

CANDIDATE
A person who is trying to get elected to a public office or job.

CENSUS
An official count of all the people in a country.

COLONY
An area of land in one country that people from another country settle in and control.

CONFEDERATION
A group of places joined together by an agreement.

CONGRESS
(1) A meeting of representatives who come together to discuss a particular matter; (2) the law-making body of the USA.

CONSTITUTION
A set of rules that state how a country is to be organized and governed.

CONVENTION
An important gathering or assembly of representatives from different places.

DEADLOCK
A situation in which no progress can be made.

DEBT
A sum of money that is owed and is to be repaid.

DELEGATE
A person sent to a meeting as a representative of a place or organization.

DIPLOMAT
An official representing a country abroad.

DRAFT
To prepare a written version of something.

DUEL
A contest between two people.

ELECTION
The process of choosing a person, especially by having a vote.

ESSAY
A short piece of writing.

FACTION
A small group of like-minded people working inside a larger group.

FEDERAL
A system of government in which individual states come under central or national authority.

INAUGURATION
When a person is formally or officially admitted to do a job.

INDEPENDENCE
When a country exists by itself and is no longer controlled by another country.

LIBERTY
When a person is free to do as he or she likes, as long as it is within the law.

PAMPHLET
A printed leaflet or booklet.

PLANTATION
An estate on which crops such as tobacco and sugar are grown.

RATIFY
To sign or give agreement to something so that it becomes official.

:BELLION

n act of armed resistance to an
stablished government or leader.

:PRESENTATIVE

person chosen to act or speak
or others.

:TIRED

When a person leaves a job and
tops working.

:DITION

n action or speech that encourages
eople to rebel against the state.

:RVEYOR

person who examines land
nd buildings.

AX

n amount of money a person
as to pay the government.

:REATY

n agreement made
etween countries.

PHOTO CREDITS

The publishers would like to thank the following sources for their kind permission to reproduce the pictures in this book.

Key: t=Top, b=Bottom, c=Centre, l=Left and r=Right.

2-3 Sergey Kamshylin/Shutterstock; 3 LOC; 4-5 Wikimedia Commons; 5t North Wind Picture Archives/akg-images; 5r Wikimedia Commons; 6-7 North Wind Picture Archives/Alamy; 6 GraphicaArtis/Corbis; 7tr INTERFOTO/Alamy; 7c Virginia Historical Society, Richmond, Virginia, USA/Bridgeman Images; 7bl Wikimedia Commons; 7br Universal History Archive/Universal Images Group/Rex Features; 8-9 Omniphoto/UIG/Bridgeman Images; 8 © Collection of the New-York Historical Society, USA/Bridgeman Images; 9l Walter Bibikow/JAI/Corbis; 9r Michael Nicholson/Corbis; 10-11 Wikimedia Commons; 10l Stock Montage/Getty Images; 11tl Wikimedia Commons; 11b Wikimedia Commons; 12-13 Wikimedia Commons; 12b White House Historical Association; 13t Private Collection; 13b Universal Images Group/Getty Images; 14-15 LOC; 14l LOC; 14r Getty Images; 15r Photo © Boltin Picture Library/Bridgeman Images; 16-17 Wikimedia Commons; 16l Galushko Sergey/Shutterstock; 16c Wikimedia Commons; 17 MPI/Getty Images; 18-19 Universal Images Group/Getty Images; 18l Kean Collection/Getty Images; 19t The Granger Collection/Topfoto; 19b Wikimedia Commons; 20–21 The Image Bank/Getty Images; 20l The Bridgeman Art Library/Getty Images; 20r Stock Montage/Getty Images; 21tl The Granger Collection/Topfoto; 21c North Wind Picture Archives/Alamy; 21br Fotosearch/Getty Images; 22-23 Bettmann/Corbis; 22l Universal Images Group/Getty Images; 22r Charles Phelps Cushing/ClassicStock/Topfoto; 23l Chicago History Museum/UIG/Getty Images; 23r The Granger Collection/Topfoto; 24l Private Collection/Peter Newark American Pictures/Bridgeman Images; 24c GraphicaArtis/Corbis; 24r The Granger Collection/Topfoto; 25l The Granger Collection/Topfoto; 25r The Granger Collection/Topfoto; 26l Wirepec/Thinkstock; 26-27 Getty Images; 27tl Wikimedia Commons; 27tr Mark Payne/Shutterstock; 27b Bettmann/Corbis; 28-29 Wikimedia Commons; 28c LOC; 28r Wikimedia Commons; 29t J Main/Shutterstock; 29b Wikimedia Commons; 30-31 The Granger Collection/Topfoto; 30l Wikimedia Commons; 30r NARA; 31l Private Collection; 32-33 NARA; 32l LOC; 33t The Granger Collection/Topfoto; 33bl LOC; 33br Topfoto; 34 LOC; 35tl LOC; 35tr LOC; 35b Private Collection; 36-37 LOC; 37l NARA; 37r LOC; 38r White House Historical Association; 38l Private Collection; 39tr LOC; 39bl LOC; 40-41 LOC; 40l LOC; 41l Wikimedia Commons; 41c LOC; 41r MPI/Stringer/Getty Images; 42-45 Wikimedia Commons.

Every effort has been made to acknowledge correctly and contact the source and/or copyright holder of each picture and Carlton Books Limited apologises for any unintentional errors or omissions, which will be, corrected in future editions of this book.

This edition published by Scholastic Inc., 557
Broadway, New York, NY 10012,
by arrangement with Carlton Books Limited.

Text, design, and illustrations © 2014
by Carlton Books Limited.
All rights reserved.

ISBN 978-0-545-77358-4
10 9 8 7 6 5 4 3 2 1   10 11 12 13 14
Printed in Dongguan, China

Senior Editor: Alexandra Koken
Design Manager: Jake da'Costa
Picture Research: Emma Copestake
Production: Charlotte Cade

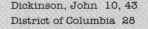

INDEX